GW00362856

The Healing POWER of Hope

TWENTY-THIRD PUBLICATIONS

185 WILLOW STREET • PO BOX 180 • MYSTIC, CT 06355
TEL: 1-800-321-0411 • FAX: 1-800-572-0788
E-MAIL: ttpubs@aol.com • www.twentythirdpublications.com

NOVALIS

Novalis
49 Front Street East, 2nd Floor
Toronto, Ontario, Canada
M5E 1B3
Phone: 1-800-387-7164 or (416) 363-3303
Fax: 1-800-204-4140 or (416) 363-9409
Email: novalis@interlog.com
ISBN: 2-89507-525-2

Twenty-Third Publications
A Division of Bayard
185 Willow Street
P.O. Box 180
Mystic, CT 06355
(860) 536-2611 or (800) 321-0411
www.twentythirdpublications.com
ISBN:1-58595-362-8

Library of Congress Catalog Card Number: 2004107166
Printed in the U.S.A.

Contents

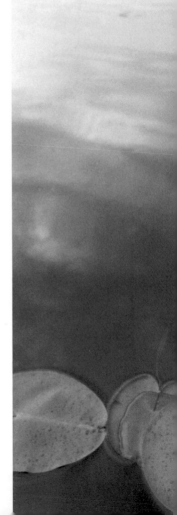

The remarkable advances of modern science and technology in recent years have awakened new hopes and expectations for the quality of human life. People today are eager to adopt new ways of thinking and behaving, and to experience greater satisfaction in their lives.

And yet, notwithstanding all this progress, we have yet to succeed in eradicating the debilitating forces of tension and frustration. We still have wars and violence of all kinds, anxieties and worries, fears and apprehensions. We still have environmental pollution, psychological neuroses, and spiritual emptiness. And we still have disappointments—a lot of them.

1

> **Hope has a crucial place in our lives.**

We now realize, after all is said and done, the one thing that never disappoints us and will never disappoint us is hope. Only hope keeps us going.

Hope has a crucial place in our lives. It is essential for our fulfillment, our sanity, and even our survival. Wherever people work, try to create something, cultivate the fields, build families, learn, teach, start an organization, write a book, pray, and engage in social and political activities, they do it because of hope. They do this because they trust the future and invest in it. They want a brighter future. They are dissatisfied with the gap that exists between what is and what might be, between the presence of injustice and the possibility of its reduction, between the reality of suffering and the desire for its alleviation. They see the goal before them. They do everything hopefully.

No matter how we describe it, hope always remains an undeniable part of human nature. We cannot live without hope, and we will never develop if we do not commit ourselves with hope to something or someone. Some people can apparently live without faith or even without love, but not without hope. Without hope we simply cannot go on. This is why poet Charles Péguy (1873-1915) could write in his famous book *The Portal of the Mystery of Hope:*

> Hope sees what has not yet been and what will be.
> She loves what has not yet been and what will be.

This is why it is she, he continues, "who moves the whole world," and "all the world works for the little girl hope." We are charmed by the way Péguy compares the three theological virtues:

> The three virtues, my creatures.
> My daughters, my children.
> Are themselves like my other creatures.
> Of the race of men.
> Faith is a loyal Wife.
> Charity is a Mother.
> An ardent mother, noble-hearted.
> Or an older sister who is like a mother.
> Hope is a little girl, nothing at all.
> Who came into the world on Christmas day just this past year.
> Who is still playing with her snowman.
> With her German fir trees painted with frost.
> And with her ox and her ass made of German wood. Painted.

And with her manger stuffed with straw that the animals don't eat.

Because they're made of wood.

And yet it's this little girl who will endure worlds.

This little girl, nothing at all.

She alone, carrying the others, who will cross worlds past.

But why are we so fascinated by hope? What is hope? What does Christian hope add to what we know about hope in general? What kind of hope does the world expect from the people of God? What is the healing effect of hope on us and on our society?

In this little book I hope that you will find answers to these questions and to others you may have, and that it will inspire you to new beginnings. As Péguy put it so well:

There is, in that which begins, a spring; roots that never return.

A departure, a childhood that is not recovered, that is never again recovered.

Now, the little girl hope

Is she who forever begins.

Hope represents the elixir of youth and well-being.

CHAPTER ONE

The "Not Yet" Experience

Always be ready to make your defense to anyone who demands from you an accounting for the hope that is in you.

☐ 1 PETER 3:15

It's strange how we keep looking for what we are not and what we do not have in the hope that, if we could only become what we are not and acquire what we do not have, we would be happy. But the truth is that we are not born to be satisfied; when we are satisfied, we most likely become

5

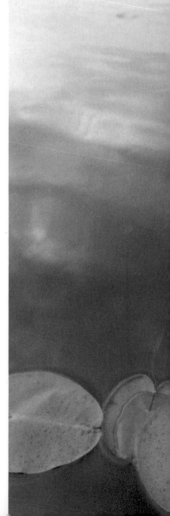

bored, and boredom can lead to self-annihilation.

The world is not yet finished, and neither are we; this is where hope comes to play a critical role in our own and others' lives. We hope to do great things which will provide great satisfaction. We yearn for sunny days and breathless starry nights. We ardently desire to experience a total communion with our loved ones. Finite beings, we long for the infinite and reject the idea that death could be the horizon of our existence.

Hope and Hopes

Hope can lead to hopes, but it does not depend on them. A person of hope can have great hopes; and even if these hopes are shattered, this individual is not shattered with them. As soon as the storm has passed, the person of hope begins to hope anew. Clement of Alexandria said: "If you do not hope, you will not find what is beyond your hopes." Our hopes, if not based on hope, will fail us. Thomas Merton described this so well when he wrote:

> If, instead of trusting in God, I trust only in my own intelligence, my own strength, and my own prudence, the means that God has given to me to find my way to him will all fail me. Nothing created is of any ultimate use without hope. To

place your trust in visible things is to live in despair.

We do not see things as they are unless we see them in the light of pure hope.

We may think that our hopes for others are in their best interests. But this is not always the case. How many parents have ruined the lives of their children because they forced their hopes on them? How many spouses have ruined their marriages because of the hopes they had for each other? How many people—even nations—have tried to control others for the sake of hopes—the hopes for a better life for them? The truth is that hopes alienate while hope liberates.

Many people have false hopes. These hopes are based on pathological denials. Consider people who have learned that they have a serious medical condition. It would be self-deluding to ignore professional opinion and construct unrealistic hopes for the future. One must face reality first.

In today's casual parlance, hope has come to mean very often a mere wish, e.g., "I hope it won't rain tomorrow," "I hope they will arrive in time for dinner," "I hope the prices will go down so I can buy a house," "I hope to win the lottery," "I tried everything, nothing left to do but hope," "Hope you have a nice day." To a question such as "Are you able to pass this test?" the answer is typically "I hope so." Let us recognize that what we often call hopes are, in fact, just good wishes. In his book *With Open Hands*, Henri Nouwen explains the difference between hope and wishes this way:

> When we live with hope we do not get tangled up with concerns for how our wishes will be fulfilled. So, too, our prayers are not directed toward the gift, but toward the one who gives it. Our prayers might still contain just as many desires, but ultimately it is not a question of having a wish come true but of expressing an unlimited faith in the giver of all good things. You wish that…but you hope for….For the prayer of hope, it is essential that there are no guarantees asked, no conditions posed, and no proofs demanded, only that you expect everything from the other without binding him in any way. Hope is based on the premise that the other gives only what is good. Hope includes an openness by which you wait for the other to make his loving promise come true, even though you never know when, where or how this might happen.

Only God can be the sure ground for a real hope. This is why we can dare to stay open to whatever happens. God is in charge.

There is a close bond between hope and imagination. Bill is in trouble. He thinks. He imagines solutions. He hypothesizes. He waits. He continues to imagine until he finds a way out. He is allowed to have expectations. But hope is not a naïve expectation in the sense that all will go smoothly. Hope is more profound than that. Hope is a certitude that God will always remain with us no matter what the circumstances.

> Only God can be the sure ground for a real hope.

Earthly hopes, when they are grounded in fundamental hope, can be a sign of God's love and a divine gift. Many of us may need happy experiences, much encouragement, and some sense of satisfaction to remain in the true path of hope. But it is when frustration strikes upon the collapse of our illusions that we often realize, it is only when we drink from the fountain of all hope—the Lord who meets our deepest desires—that our thirst is really quenched. "Those who drink of the water I give them," says the Lord, "will never be thirsty" (Jn 4:14).

Hope is essential to the human heart. Author William F. Lynch, S.J., wrote in his book *Images of Hope*: "Hope comes close to being the very heart and center of a human being." Don't we move toward recovery the minute after a disaster has struck? Instantly, we struggle to survive and be well again. The radiance of hope is a very powerful energy. Hope is life. Life is hope.

We should be prisoners of hope, as the expression goes, and not prisoners of hopes. Prisoners of hope ask, "Why not?" instead of "Why?" President John F. Kennedy once observed rightly: "Some men see things as they are and ask 'Why?' I dream things that never were and ask, 'Why not?'" These people refuse to settle for anything less than what they hope for. They can be angry with the way things are and, moreover, have the courage to change things and to be agents of change. Hope is a formidable energy.

We very often take hope for granted, and we don't appreciate it until we are in a hopeless situation. As G.K. Chesterton observed: "As long as matters are really hopeful, hope is a mere flattery or platitude; it is only when everything is hopeless that hope begins to be a strength at all. Like all the Christian virtues, it is as unreasonable as it is indispensable."

The distinction between human hope and primordial hope is clearer in French, which uses *espoir* for the former and *espérance* for the latter. The reasons for having *espoir* are usually exterior to ourselves, while the reasons for having *espérance* have their roots in the very core of who and what we are.

Hope should never be mistaken for mere optimism.

Optimism vs. Hope

Sometimes we think that hope is a kind of natural optimism. We picture the person of hope as one who invariably sees the half-full glass, and who believes that everything will always turn out right in the end. But as we all know, this is not always the case. Things can go wrong, and we have no power over this.

Optimism is a matter of temperament more than it is a virtue. Hope is a virtue; it goes beyond optimism.

Optimism tends to underestimate the power of evil and ambiguity in the world and enables one to ignore them. Hope, on the other hand, recognizing the half-empty glass as well as the half-full, grapples with the ambiguity of existence, and responds to it by imagining new possibilities, finding new alternatives, and taking new steps to implement them. It is especially in the experience of suffering—not in the denial of it—that we can reach out in hope toward true healing. Philosopher Gabriel Marcel (1889-1973) wrote in his book *Homo Viator: Introduction to a Metaphysics of Hope:* "The truth is that there can strictly be no hope except when the temptation to despair exists. Hope is the art by which this temptation is actively or victoriously overcome."

Moreover, we can say that hope is realistic because it is closer to humility than optimism and pessimism are. It is only when we fully embrace our humanity that we are able to be down-to-earth and laugh about ourselves.

Hopeful people do not pretend.

Optimists and pessimists often lack a genuine appreciation of reality as it is. Optimists and pessimists pretend. Hopeful people do not pretend. They do not simply say that everything will be all right or that the sky will fall. They go about their business without fear, without too many expectations, without self-congratulation, and without self-pity.

They do not suppress their feelings of self-worth and happiness. They do not interpret their successes as failures or their shortcomings as barriers and insurmountable obstacles. They do what they have to do, as a mother does. A mother does not make lists, does not pretend, and does not count. She loves the baby, does what love tells her to do, and watches her baby and her hope grow. She is allowed to dream.

We Are Dreamers

We're all daydreamers, aren't we? We have the imagination that provides us with the capacity to create. Our minds are equipped with the power of imagining new realities. Our intuitions see the new reality that is hidden from the eyes. We create things that did not exist before. We create art, literature, science, stories, legends, myths, ideas, visions, systems, ideologies. Dreams affect and empower activities.

Inventions start with a dream. Discoveries start with a dream. Immigrations start with a dream. Space exploration starts with a dream. Changes in a social system start with a dream. Everyone remembers the famous "I have a dream…" speech of Martin Luther King, Jr. We all have our own American dream, not only for wealth, but for health, wisdom, happiness, and holiness.

Daydreaming is rooted in the very core of the human psyche. It seems to be part of human nature. It is a basic need expressed in ways suited to particular religions, cultures, times, and places.

Do you remember Aladdin's story? In the well-known *Book of One Thousand and One Nights*, this little boy, Aladdin, manages to obtain a ring and a magic lamp. When the ring and lamp are rubbed, a jinn (genie) appears and grants any dream, wish, or request. Aladdin eventually becomes immensely wealthy, builds a wonderful palace, and marries the daughter of the sultan. He lives a happy life and, when the sultan dies, he succeeds him and reigns for many years.

Dreaming—hoping for something to happen—is magical. If you don't know what you want, ask your dreams. Do you dream about a new car, a boat, new clothes, a vacation, a promotion, less stress, a cure? Do you dream about taking a new course at the community college, running for office, working to combat illiteracy, having better relationships, being closer to God, discerning God's will? Ask your dreams.

Know exactly what you want. See it coming your way through the magical eye of hope. Hope can take you anywhere you want to go. Aladdin's magic lamp is a universal story. And always remember Michelangelo's line: "The greatest danger for most of us is not that our aim is too high and we miss it, but that it is too low and we reach it."

Michelangelo Buonarroti (1475-1564), the great

Italian sculptor, painter, architect, and poet, was still doing what he loved to do at the age of eighty-nine years, when the normal life expectancy was about forty. A dream, a high aim, and hope fuel the energy for doing extraordinary things. Michelangelo saw the statue of David in the marble, and all he had to do was to chip away the excess to allow David to take shape. Lying on his back and working every day for about four years, this great artist painted the ceiling of the Sistine Chapel.

A dream… and hope fuel the energy for doing extraordinary things.

High dreams and hope help us to heal our lives and to create our own masterpieces, whether they are symphonies or functional cooking pots. Michelangelo was right in insisting that it is more dangerous for us to have low expectations for ourselves than to have high aims and ideals. However, high aims and expectations should not be confused with unrealistic fantasy. High aims motivate us without denying reality. Mere fantasy makes us fool ourselves into hoping to escape the dreary reality of life. A purely fictitious fantasy confounds reality in its very roots. It provides excuses for not changing and growing. Excuses are so easy to find, aren't they? But for how long can one fool oneself? For how long?

Every situation involves a risk. Sometimes we will lose; sometimes we will win. The only guarantee against losing is to stay out of the game. Who can afford to do that? The only guarantee of winning is to let authentic hope lead our steps in the right direction, and to try again and again.

The Already/Not Yet Tension

Wittingly or unwittingly, we experience the already here as well as the not yet of life. But we never seem to experience a resolution of the tension between the two. A horizon in the not yet will become—in the already—a step toward another horizon. This tells about the very nature of our being, which is to be constantly on a pilgrimage or journey. We are always on the way. Always.

There is tension in hope!

The not yet is the unrealized potential within every one of us and within our world. This not yet consciousness effects through the power of imagination an eagerness for a change and stimulates the hope of the human heart to carry out what was longed for. Is getting there all that matters? Maybe it is for some of us, until another horizon shows up. History teach us that things are never finally resolved. Searching is part of the game of life. Settling down, except for a moment of rest, would end the search and the game. Hope, with its powerful ability to transcend the present and its obvious limitations, opens the door to other possibilities and other realities.

It is basic for understanding the pilgrim's way to be aware of the dialectical dynamics of the already/not yet approach. Common sense tells us that when things are meaningful to us, they are already but not totally (not yet) meaningful. We do not find meaning as we find a lost pencil. Meaning is always new, always growing, and always refreshing.

Meaning, when we keep looking, expands. The horizon shifts when we move to the line we thought was the horizon. The possible has no fixed frontiers. We are wired to explore all possible avenues. We hope that our hope will guarantee the success of getting there. Hope is our passion for the possible, and the possible has no limits. This is true for our physical life, and this is true—even more so—for our spiritual life. As we read in the letter of John: "We are God's children now [already]; what we will be has not yet been revealed [not yet] (1 Jn 3:2).

We still have long way to go. We are just pilgrims on the road. We live in time. We remember the past, we see the present, and we move toward the future. All our predictions and expectations indicate how eager we are to know this future and try to master it. Hope leads the way.

To be hopeful and to be directed toward the future in all its openness, despite its frustrations and setbacks, is what makes us more human and more divine. Hope liberates us, invigorates us, and transforms us by giving meaning to our lives.

> Hope liberates us, invigorates us, and transforms us.

All of us, knowingly or unknowingly, seek to give meaning to our lives. Who does not need a reason for existing? Thus we search in the varieties of human experience for this reason. We try to find meaning in the family, social life, professional life, or in any other sphere we feel drawn to. However, sooner or later, we will reach a point where we realize that we have not yet discovered the real meaning of life. Not yet.

The content of the not yet must come from a different order. We realize that it is the divine consciousness—"The mind of Christ" (1 Cor 2:16)—that gives real meaning to our lives. We know it because neither a family, nor a profession, nor money, nor social position, has ever truly and fully satisfied us. It is only when we work for the coming of the reign of God that we realize the true meaning of life. We never feel alone, abandoned, or depressed after that, because we are working in the Lord's vineyard.

The truth is that if we spend our time complaining about not having enough money, time, friends, or opportunities to succeed, we demonstrate that we have not yet discovered the meaning of our lives. When we grasp the "only one thing" (Lk 10:42) that is necessary, everything else will become secondary. In comparison to the one thing, everything else pales. Hope surpasses all other hopes.

It is interesting to notice how hope was expressed in different ways throughout the ages. Remember, for example, the story of Ponce de Leon (1460-1521), who went searching for the fountain of perpetual youth. Remember the eagerness of the alchemists searching for a solvent that could turn base metal into gold (the philosopher's stone). Remember the story of David slaying the giant, a story that opens the door for the weak person to dream of possible victory.

Remember the fairy tales, and the supermen and superwomen who arrive just in time to put things right. All these stories, images, and intimations point to the fact that there is, in our human nature, an unmistakable vivid hope. This hope is even more evident in the gospel, which is the good news of God's love and our redemption. This hope, by which we are saved, provides the assurance of ultimate victory.

What are our most urgent needs in life? Really, not much, if we think about it. Just fresh air and water, and some bread. However, we need a lot of hope. Hope keeps rejuvenating us until we become new beings. No wonder we hear the word "new" at every turn: a new philosophy, a new diet, a new science, a new interpretation, a new way of thinking, a new product, a new heaven and earth, a new "you." The book of Genesis tells us that we are created in the image of God. If we truly believe this, we must also believe that a divine future awaits us. Hope is the magical force that shapes and realizes this future reality. And this will be our ever-ancient and ever-new reality.

At the present time, we are entering a critical moment in the history of humanity—a time of great opportunity as well as a time of great peril. We also observe that, in this most stressful, pivotal, and exciting time, a true movement of spiritual revival is beginning to take place all over the world. This movement, which is the fruit of a higher consciousness our human race has reached, will produce consequences that will shape the present and reverberate far into the future. We are on duty to build a new earth—a healthy earth, a prosperous earth, an earth enlivened by God's blessings. No other choice is possible, for the only alternative would be total annihilation. Hope is the grounded ideal that points the way for this renewal movement to reach its full bloom.

FOR YOUR REFLECTION & RESPONSE

1. Enter a quiet room. You are alone, surrounded by silence. Write all the hopes you have with respect to a particular project. Now imagine for a moment something has happened and all your hopes are dashed. Assess your deep feeling of despair. Observe the hope that is left, the hope rooted in your soul and heart. Can you identify it and describe it? Does anything get in the way and prevent you from maintaining a sense of hope? Does hope motivate you to work for change in your world, even at a high cost? Does your hope in God allow you to act even within the circumstances you may not be able to change?

2. Farmers hope to feed you and me. When they plant something, they see more than is visible. If you have some space behind the house, plant a seed, and watch how it evolves and grows. Isn't farming and gardening an act of hope?

3. Parenting and teaching are true acts of hope, even though we may not think about them this way. Aren't we raising children so they will have a better future and, in so doing, assure the world of a better future too? Spend some time with lit-

tle children today. See in them the world-to-be, and act with them as you wish that world to be.

4. Tonight, before you go to bed, review your day. Did your activities reflect what you hoped for? Were your time, effort, and achievements directed toward the goal you hoped to accomplish? Do you feel insecure in some areas of your life? Does anything confound your hope? Can you imagine a situation in your own life in which something that looks impossible can be changed by hope? Do you have an image of yourself for the distant future? How comfortable are you with seeing this image?

5. Do the people you meet take their leave of you with more hope in their hearts? Do your friends and the members of your family feel that, perhaps because of you, they want, in their own individual ways, to contribute to the communities to which they belong and to the world at large? Are you clear about what you most hope for yourself and for the world? Do you know what God wants you to become?

AFFIRMATION

Repeat this several times a day.

Hope is the light of my life.

PRAYER

Dear God, through the many hopes I have, uncover the lack of my in-depth knowledge of myself and of the destination to which I am heading. I am sure of one thing, though. I am not lost, for my hope in you allows me to place my life and my future in your care.

I hope I will never do anything that is not in your plan for me. I hope to be able to do whatever I do according to your will. I hope my not yet becomes my already.

Almighty God, make my longing for you increase day after day. Strengthen my hope in you as well as your hope in me. Open my eyes to see hope everywhere today and every day. You are my hope. Amen.

CHAPTER TWO

The Dimensions of Christian Hope

Hope does not disappoint us, because God's love has been poured into our hearts through the Holy Spirit that has been given to us.

ROM 5:5

Do we need reasons to hope? Or do we hope without regard for reasons, or even with reasons that compel us not to hope at all (the "Hoping against hope" of Rom 4:18)?

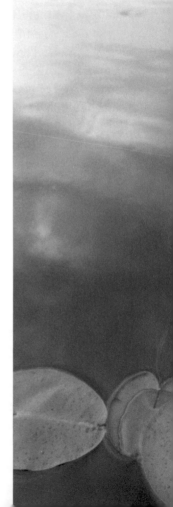

25

Our small hopes—important as they may be—are in the end trivial if they are not related to the radical faith in God and the hope that the Creator endows creation with a future.

The biblical promises of God and Christian thought throughout the centuries underline the importance of hope and its creative power in shaping our unfulfilled selves and our unfinished world.

The Bible as a Book of Hope

The Scriptures can be considered the record of the story of hope. Everything in the Bible seems oriented toward it. The Old and New Testaments are promise and fulfillment. "The promises of God," wrote theologian Jürgen Moltmann, "disclose the horizons of history." The Bible describes God at work within history—our own history—toward a future in which all things will be made new.

God promised Abraham to make of him a great nation, that he would be blessed and that he would become a blessing (see Gen 12). God showed continued fidelity to this promise despite the many disloyalties of God's people. As far as Abraham himself is concerned, St. Paul says that "Hoping against hope, he (Abraham) believed that he would become 'the father of many nations'" (Rom 4:18). Abraham's life was truly an exercise of hope.

Job, who "was blameless and upright, one who feared God and turned away from evil" (Job 1:1), was quickly stripped of all he held dear, including wealth, position, health, and family, and left utterly alone. Yet Job, bereft and derelict, maintained a theology of hope and confessed his faith, "For I know that my Redeemer lives, and that at the last he will stand upon the earth; and after my skin has been thus destroyed, then in my flesh I shall see God" (Job 19:25–26). Job saw beyond his present suffering. No trial is too difficult when one hopes that the living Redeemer will write the final chapter.

The prophets repeated this promise, especially to David (see 2 Sam 7:9, 16). Jeremiah predicted disaster for the people because of their sins, but he also promised that the people would return to safety: "For I am with you, says the Lord, to save you" (Jer 30:11).

Ezekiel warned of the destruction coming upon Jerusalem, but then delivered the promises of restoration: "Thus says the Lord God: I am going to open your graves, and bring you from your graves, O my people.… I will put my spirit within you, and you shall live, and I will place you on your own soil; then you shall know that I, the Lord, have spoken and will act, says the Lord" (Ezek 37:12–14).

According to Jewish law, Hosea could have divorced his adulterous wife. But God told him to keep his wife and renew his vows to her. This is precisely the lesson that God wanted to convey to Israel: God would remain faithful even though the people were unfaithful.

> How can I give you up, Ephraim? How can I hand you over, O Israel?... My heart recoils within me; my compassion grows warm and tender. I will not execute my fierce anger; I will not again destroy Ephraim; for I am God and no mortal, the Holy One in your midst, and I will not come in wrath (Hos 11:8–9).

The point here is to recognize God's part of the bargain. God is faithful. God is consistent. God is not only the God of the Promised Land. God is also the God of the journey, the milk, the honey, the familiar, the unfamiliar, the risk, and the homecoming. God honors commitments. We can be sure that we will never be disappointed if we base our hope on the divine steadfastness. We're right to count on God. God is with us, within us, among us, and around us. This is why the mystic Julian of Norwich (1342-1416) can say: "All shall be well, and all shall be well, and all manner of thing shall be well."

Now we understand why Paul makes a point of affirming: "If for this life only we have hoped in Christ, we are of all people most to be pitied. But in fact Christ has been raised from the dead" (1 Cor 15:19–20). Therefore we will never be disappointed, and with Christ everything is possible. So we can live by hope.

Peter has been called the apostle of hope because after denying his relationship to Jesus three times, he did not despair of God's mercy the way Judas did. He renewed his hope and returned to Jesus. This Peter, known as the rock, wrote: "By his great mercy [God] has given us a new birth into a living hope through the resurrection of Jesus Christ from the dead, and into an inheritance that is imperishable, undefiled, and unfading, kept in heaven for you" (1 Pet 1:3–4). This future inheritance that Peter is talking about is the object of Christian hope. And Christian hope is focused on Jesus Christ, who is our hope.

Scholar and author Father Bernard Häring wrote in his book *Hope Is the Remedy*:

> Christian hope is focused on Jesus Christ.

Christ is our hope as the fulfillment of God's saving love, God's saving mercy and God's saving justice. God is our hope as the great sacrament, the great visible sign of God's fidelity and love for all men. Christ is our hope as victor over all evil powers, over frustration, over sin, over solidarity in sinfulness and selfishness, over anguish and death. Christ is our hope as the risen Lord; he is the new creation. He is the final Word of God to man, the last and final prophet promised to those who believe in him and are truly his disciples.

Christ is the one who has come and who is coming, the one who is the great sacrament of hope from whom all other sacraments, events, and signs receive meaning and direction. He is the one who permeates our world and transforms it. He is the one who will hand everything, and himself, to the Father. For this reason, hope is a structural element of Christian life and of human existence; life is given to the dead, and the things that do not exist, exist (see Rom 4:17).

> Hope is a structural element of Christian life and of human existence.

Let's face it. The gospel of the crucified and risen Christ is meaningless if it is not the answer to the human quest for a fulfilled life. The reign of God on earth that is revealed in Jesus Christ is the very reason for our hope, because he is "the way, and the truth, and the life" (Jn 14:6). Christ is the center of everything. He is all in all. He is the beginning and the end of history and the way in between. For this kind of hope we can endure anything. Think about the long list of martyrs and saints of the Church. Remember Paul's account of his tribulations:

> Five times I have received from the Jews the forty lashes minus one. Three times I was beaten with rods. Once I received a stoning. Three times I was shipwrecked; for a night and a day I was adrift at sea; on frequent journeys, in danger from rivers, danger from bandits, danger from my own people, danger from Gentiles, danger in the city, danger in the wilderness, danger at sea, danger from false brothers and sisters; in toil and hardship, through many a sleepless night, hungry and thirsty, often without food, cold and naked. And, besides other things, I am under daily pressure because of my anxiety for all the churches (2 Cor 11:24–28).

These are daunting trials, are they not? But in spite of all these adversities, he is moved by hope. As Paul writes elsewhere:

> Who will separate us from the love of Christ? Will hardship, or distress, or persecution, or famine, or nakedness, or peril, or sword?...I am convinced that neither death, nor life, nor angels, nor rulers, nor things present nor things to come nor powers, nor height, nor depth, nor anything else in all creation, will be able to separate us from the love of God in Christ Jesus our Lord (Rom 8:35, 38–39).

This tension between the greatness of God and our human misery prompted thinker and writer Blaise Pascal (1623-1662) to write:

> The knowledge of God without that of man's misery causes pride. The knowledge of man's misery without that of God causes despair. The knowledge of Jesus Christ constitutes the middle course, because in him we find both God and our misery.

Hope, then, becomes, for Christ's disciples, a definite personal relationship. And no matter what will befall Christ's disciples, they know that "God will wipe away every tear from their eyes" (Rev 7:17; also 21:4).

Christian Hope

Christian hope is not just mere longing. We can have it only as God's gift. It is rooted in the mystery of the Triune God. Indeed, the Father in whom we are created and to whom we are heading is the "God of hope" (Rom 15:13). The Son who is our "Way" (Jn 14:6) of life is the perfect symbol of hope, because those who travel on that "new and living way" (Heb 10:20) "abound in hope by the power of the Holy Spirit" (Rom 15:13). This kind of hope will never disappoint us.

Paul affirms that "Suffering produces endurance, and endurance produces character, and character produces hope, and hope does not disappoint us, because God's love has been poured into our hearts through the Holy Spirit that has been given to us" (Rom 5:3–5). We live by this gift of hope as Thomas Aquinas wrote, "No man is able by himself to grasp the supreme good of eternal life; he needs divine help. Hence there is here a twofold object, the eternal life we hope for, and the divine help we hope by."

Even though Christian hope rests on what is affirmed by faith, it is in the weakness of this faith, we can say, that hope has a better chance to flourish. Real hope does not always count on assurances coming from understanding God's plans for us, nor from the consolation of feeling the closeness of God, nor even from the certainty of doing God's will.

Real hope is openness to the active presence of God that can be manifested in visible and felt actions, or in the experience of absence or complete darkness. This is probably what prompted theologian Karl Rahner to say, "Hope hopes God." This affirmation goes further than hoping in God or for God. Hoping God is the point. Nothing more, nothing less. Unconditional hope, unconditional trust, unconditional confidence.

Charles Péguy's *The Portal of the Mystery of Hope* describes this attitude as a surprise.

> The faith that I love the best, says God, is hope.
> Faith doesn't surprise me. It's not surprising….
> Charity, says God, that doesn't surprise me.
> It's not surprising….
> But hope, says God, that is something that surprises me.
> Even me.
> That is surprising.

Christian hope has several distinctive dimensions. Christian hope is based on the teachings and praxis of Jesus, especially with regard to the reign of God, and to his relationship with the Father and the Holy Spirit and with us.

Christian hope is rooted in the historic crucifixion and resurrection of Christ. By acknowledging this historical reality, hope acknowledges at the same time the reality of death and resurrection, darkness and light, sadness and joy, suffering and wellness, sickness and good health as intrinsic elements of Christian existence.

Because it is founded on Jesus' words, "Heaven and earth will pass away, but my words will not pass away" (Mt 24:35), Christian hope transcends place, time, cultures, circumstances, and personal opinions. In a comprehensive way, it embraces the realities of this world and those beyond, the present and the future, the prophetic and apocalyptic. Thus, if we try to separate Christian hope from worldly hope, we risk misunderstanding not only the teachings of Jesus, but also the theological significance of the mystery of his incarnation, death, and resurrection.

Jesus, by identifying with our flesh and blood, declares his readiness to meet us wherever there is human creativity and joy, as well as human need and despair. We encounter Christ in the midst of our

> Christian hope is a dynamic creative energy because it relies on the flow of the grace of God.

ordinary realities—the joys, the ambiguities, the compromises, the illnesses, and the uncertainties of life. His gift is himself. We don't rest except in him.

"May the God of hope fill you with all joy and peace in believing, so that you may abound in hope by the power of the Holy Spirit" (Rom 15:13). And we know that, in order to keep hope alive in this uncertain world, the cost was and still is God on the cross. The God of hope confounds all our conflicts, narrow-mindedness, and pettinesses.

Christian hope is a dynamic creative energy because it relies on the flow of the grace of God. Peacemaking, for example, is not, in a Christian perspective, a simple political strategy or a technique one can learn from a book or from life experience. Peacemaking is based on a deep union with God and on the trust that those who walk with God walk in peace. This means that there is a price to pay, the price of discipleship that will require us to launch an assault against the principalities and powers of this world, and the recognition that in and of ourselves we cannot win. But with the Lord, all things are possible, and he will make all things new as he promised.

The new creation, the not yet, which is on the way to becoming the already, will involve a radical refashioning of our consciousness. We have to put on the mind of Christ (see 1 Cor 2:16; Eph 6:11; Gal 3:27) and see the world as he sees it. The Chinese proverb, "Most of what we see comes from behind the eyes," aptly describes the new reality. Genuine Christian hope is able to transform our perception, which in turn transforms our ways of being in the world and. in the process, the world itself. In this sense, Christian hope can be called out of this world, not in some kind of fanciful utopia, but in an unbelievable reality never seen before.

When Jesus talked about the reign of God, he did not mean some philosophical utopia; rather, he was describing the way to make heaven on earth, and sketching a road map to achieve that goal. Hope enables us to see God in all things, and calls attention to our responsibility for contributing to God's work in this world. So it is not accurate to think of Christian hope as an escape mechanism. John Macquarrie describes this error in his book *Christian Hope*:

In the popular understanding—or misunderstanding—of it, Christian hope has come to be visualized almost entirely in other worldly terms. Thus, to the sceptic, Christian hope looks like an escape mechanism or comforting illusion. It is cynically described as pie in the sky and seen as a tranquillizer which diverts attention and energy from the problems of our actual existence and so lessens the hope that these problems might be overcome.

Christian hope is not escape, but full engagement. It underlines our responsibility for the world. In no way can we seek our salvation and ignore the rest of men and women who do not belong to the club. No one can make the journey to God in a solitary and selfish manner. No one is an island. No one can *be* an island. Good or bad, we make a difference in the world.

The Second Vatican Council, especially in *Gaudium et Spes* (Joy and Hope): *Pastoral Constitution on the Church in the Modern World*, emphatically states that "A hope related to the end of time does not diminish the importance of intervening duties, but rather undergirds the acquittal of them with fresh incentives" (21; see also 34, 38, 39).

Further, this same constitution talks about the internal relationship and unity between hope for the world to come and hope for this life. It says: "Christians, on pilgrimage toward the heavenly city, should seek and savor the things which are above. This duty in no way decreases, but rather increases, the weight of their obligation to work with all men in constructing a more human world" (57). Consequently, Christian hope is restless, apostolic, always on the go, to the ends of the earth, as Jesus commanded.

Building the secular city is one of our duties. Don't we acknowledge this intention everyday by repeating: "Your kingdom come, your will be done on earth as it is in heaven"? If we do not believe in this prayer, and if we do not hope to change the things around us, we must conclude that Christianity has nothing to offer humanity in its present predicament. But we know that all things must be restored in Christ. We pray in hope, and by exercising this prayerful hope we are critical of everything that already is, longing for God's reign, the only lasting institution there is.

Jürgen Moltmann, the champion of hope and author of *The Theology of Hope*, observes:

Faith, wherever it develops into hope, causes not rest but unrest, not patience but impatience. It does not calm the unquiet heart, but is itself this unquiet heart in man. Those who hope in Christ can no longer put up with reality as it is, but begin to suffer under it, to contradict it. Peace with God means conflict with the world, for the goad of the promised future stabs inexorably into the flesh of every unfulfilled present. If we had before our eyes only what we see, then we should cheerfully or reluctantly reconcile ourselves with things as they happen to be. That we do not reconcile ourselves, that there is no pleasant harmony between us and reality, is due to our unquenchable hope. This hope keeps man unreconciled, until the great day of the fulfillment of all the promise of God.

By the way, Christian hope cannot be equated with conservative or liberal political viewpoints. Christian hope is concerned with God's reign, no matter whom one votes for.

If we want to avoid frustration and disappointment, our hope should be placed in God, not in the people of God, for only "Jesus Christ is the same yesterday and today and forever" (Heb 13:8). How shallow and transient any human conception appears when seen in the perspective of the eternal Word of God!

Christian hope helps pull things together and integrates the heavenly city and the secular city. It also integrates what was, what is, and what can be. Consequently, it leads to great challenges and changes such as the development of political, liberation, and ecological theologies, as well as the emerging effort to find the radical unity that exists between the mystical and political, contemplation and action, liberation and salvation, justice and peace, the within and the without, and adversity and healing.

> Christian hope cannot be equated with conservative or liberal political viewpoints.

Hope allows us to see in human history God's action for healing, growth, and fulfillment. But let us make sure that we trust in God, not simply in our concept or image or limited understanding of God. God is greater than our knowledge of him. The truth is that what we find as a result of our searching hopes is not what we are looking for, but what we are looking after—our true self in God. Then everything will fall into place. Then we understand the slogan: *Spes quaerens intellectum—spero, ut intellegam* (Hope seeking understanding—I hope, in order that I may understand). This kind of hope is not individual and private only; it is also the general hope of the whole of the creation.

True hope comes from the word of God, not from the speculations of theologians. It is, as the *Catechism of the Catholic Church* defines it, "The theological virtue by which we desire the kingdom of heaven and eternal life as our happiness, placing our trust in Christ's promises and relying not on our own strength, but on the help of the grace of the Holy Spirit" (No. 1817).

How Great Is Your Hope?

If "Christ Jesus [is] our hope" (1 Tim 1:1), our hope should be as great as Christ himself—unlimited. And since Christ is all in all, he embodies every hope we have and exhausts all we can even know about God. He is our focus as he is God's Son. He is our fullness as he dwells within us. He is our fulfillment as he carries out his purposes through us.

The world is currently facing extraordinary challenges and crises demanding radical and comprehensive solutions. There is a patent advance of secularism, religious relativism, politicization of religious beliefs, religious zealotry, religious-based terrorism, fanaticism, and a new paganism that proclaims no fixed truth, no enduring definitions, no final reference for what is good, no ultimate meaning or purpose. There are also economic, political, and social challenges of all kinds.

Only hope in God's ways can truly change things, cure our moral paralysis, and deliver the world from its powerlessness, dereliction, dullness, and sin. God is committed to transform us into a more perfect manifestation of Christ's body. Our hope has a missionary dimension. It is to be proclaimed everywhere. Our hope restores, heals, and liberates. Our hope has no limits, because it demonstrates the presence and activity of God in the world through Christ.

In this sense, hope is not only a theological virtue, but also a social virtue—a virtue that is, precisely because of its theological nature, socially dangerous. It invites us to the possibilities of transformation and radical change. Imagine the consequences, when our eyes are focused on God. Then "[t]here is no longer Jew or Greek, there is no longer slave or free, there is no longer male and female; for all of you are one in Christ Jesus" (Gal 3:28). No one and nothing is excluded.

Filled with God's light and hope, we truly become the light and hope of the world.

For Your Reflection & Response

1. We have all been disappointed many times. Things go wrong. People fail. Expectations come to naught. Now what? Go to the nearest church and light a candle, or light one in your home. No darkness can resist the flame of this little candle. No adversity can resist a glimmer of hope.

2. There is an old adage: "I was waiting for someone to do something, and then I realized I was that someone." Today, sow some grains of hope. Help someone in need. Do not wait for someone else to begin, and do not concern yourself with results.

3. Is it hard for you to believe that God has a plan for you—a plan that, when carried out, contributes in the transformation of the world? What do you see on your horizon? What is the future of God in your life? Do you believe human history has a goal toward which it is heading? Where do you see your place in that history?

4. Take a walk in nature. Listen to the songbirds, and enjoy the sight of a beautiful blooming flower. Notice how grasses grow around a rock. Take in the fragrances of the field. Stretch your

arms and touch the branch of a tree. Take a deep, deep, deep breath of fresh air. On this day, without knowing it, you've read one of the most inspiring books of hope. On this day, you've prayed an act of hope in the Creator.

5. What do you hope for as a Christian? Do you hope to be with God primarily in heaven and only secondarily on this earth? Does the eschatological perspective affect, in your own mind, issues such as the relationship between prayer and politics, faith and justice, peace and war, religions and the social mission of the Church, contemplation and action, ethics and realism, the not yet and the already realities? Do you see ambiguity and contradiction in these terms? What is your picture of the better world you hope for?

6. Everyone asks, in one way or another, the same questions because we all share the same origin and the same destiny. "Where do we come from?" "Why are we here?" "Where are we going?" Bearing in mind your hoped-for destination, please answer the question, "What is next in your life?" Then answer this one, "What practical steps will you take to live your hope?"

Affirmation

Say this several times a day.

God is my true hope.

Prayer

Dear God, your beatitudes (see Mt 5:3–12) tell me that my tough times belong to future blessings. Help me to bear adequately my tough times and also the cost of the possibilities and blessings coming my way. I hope. Despair would be easier in tough times. But I hope.

Through the hope you provided me, my world will change. This hope transforms my tough times so that they are tough no longer. The hope you gave me allows me to live my life according to the values that you teach. Now, my life has a future. It has a future because I hope in you. It is a future I do not see. Who cares? You are with me. You are my hope.

Dear Lord, since you never disappoint me, help me to never disappoint you. Amen.

CHAPTER THREE

Doctor Hope

Uphold me according to your promise, that I may live, and let me not be put to shame in my hope.

☐ PSALMS 119:116

Have you known people who, as soon as they retire, die? Have you known others who feel constantly tired and sleep until mid-morning, then spend the rest of the day watching television? Have you known people who no longer smile because they are depressed?

All these people most likely suffer from lack of hope. Some retired people, when they no

47

longer have a job and no longer feel needed, die. Those who do not have goals to motivate them are always tired. Those who do not find meaning in their lives are depressed.

Hope is the remedy for many of these illnesses.

Impact of Hope on Health

Medical literature is filled with stories of patients who, because of their hope, were completely healed or at least lived longer than expected. Researchers, especially in the field of psychoneuroimmunology, have found that thoughts and emotions have a great influence on the body. So, an attitude like that of hope, which embodies thought and emotion, has a direct effect on the immune system and even on the individual organs of the body. This is why it is so important to foster a positive attitude in patients.

Dr. Stephen Nordlicht, a clinical associate professor of psychiatry at Cornell University Medical School, has reported in an article in the *New York State Journal of Medicine*: "How we speak to the patient, the vocabulary we use, the time we select to do this can all serve to either strengthen the patient or weaken him." And he adds that "hope, which is inherent in every human being, will have to be utilized as a medical instrument to a much greater degree than in the past." Yale oncologist Dr. Bernie Siegel says,

If there's one thing I learned from my years of working with cancer patients, it's that there is no such thing as false hope. Hope is real and physiological. It's something I feel perfectly comfortable giving people—no matter what their situation. I know people are alive today because I said to them, "You don't have to die."

Indeed, who can pretend to know enough to be a pessimist?

Dr. Isaac Djerassi, director of research oncology at Mercy Catholic Medical Center in Philadelphia and one of the world's leading authorities on cancer, underlines the importance of hope with these words:

I can say from my own experience that patients who have given up, who have come to me feeling defeated and desperate, feeling that nothing can possibly help them, have often made their own prediction come true. The fighter-type patients who are willing to try anything that has a chance to help them, who have real faith in their survival, always do better. The same thing holds true of doctors. Some of the doctors get

A more positive and hopeful attitude makes all the difference.

ℬ

discouraged too early and give up on patients who could still be helped. When you pick a doctor, make certain he's a fighter, someone who will stand by you and fight for you.

There are hundreds of reports that attest to improvements in patients' health—even among those who are terminally ill—when these patients find something new to live for. Shifting to a more positive and hopeful attitude makes all the difference. We must say that, as others studies have shown, helpless and hopeless people have a greater risk of developing cancer and other serious diseases. Why? Because these terrible diseases become the response to an ontological weakness, where patients no longer desire anything but sleep and death.

Patients do not usually reach this point overnight. If hope can be built in steps, it can be destroyed in steps too. One setback is isolation. Long-term illness often results in a person being hospitalized or confined to a health care facility, separated from family, friends, co-workers, and normal routines. Loneliness hits home. Then the patient cannot but feel that life goes on without him or her.

Another setback is loss of identity. When mothers can no longer mother, fathers can no longer father, teachers can no longer teach, nurses can no longer nurse, and—worse—when they are identified by numbers, patients usually tend to lose their own identity and become confused about their mission in life—if they have one. Such a situation can easily lead to a loss of interest in life and, consequently, to irritability, sleeplessness, and depression.

Another setback is hopelessness. Hopelessness, according to the North American Nursing Diagnosis Association, is defined as "the subjective state in which an individual feels that alternatives and personal choices are limited or nonexistent, resulting in an inability to mobilize energy." Hopelessness has warning signs that include apathy, indifference, passivity, emotional numbness, withdrawal from others and from social activities, and decreased appetite.

Another particularly alarming sign is a frantic hyperactivity in which one lives like there's no tomorrow and immerses himself or herself totally in the distractions, benefits, and the pleasures of the moment at hand. This kind of narcotic hedonism, which focuses on illusory goals, is bound to give way sooner or later to a deep sense of futility and afflictions, including serious illness.

It is obvious that when someone gives up, he or she is paving the way to illness and various troubles. Life is not meant to be lived this way. Hopelessness without end should be replaced by endless hope.

Making Hope Work for You

Hope is a belief, feeling, and attitude that has caught the attention of the medical world, which sees in it the possibility of healing even terminal diseases. Hope is powerful medicine indeed.

There is an eighty-five-year-old woman in my neighborhood who has experienced more tribulations and suffering than anyone else I've known. Let us call her Ann. Neither I nor my neighbors ever heard Ann complain about anything. No trace of bitterness in her heart. No unresolved arguments in her mind. No unforgiving thoughts in her soul; just a radiant attitude of peace and joy.

I asked her once what kept her going in spite of all the adversities she encountered in her life. She remained silent for a moment before replying, "Well, I hoped things were going to be better, but when my life is over, I'll be happy with God in heaven." Ann's reply was neither an academic rationalization nor a

pat response she had learned by rote some sixt
before. She uttered the truth of a lifetime of exp..r
ence. Her response to me meant that, when our
hopes are shattered, one can either go into a state of
depression and despair, or one can develop a radical
hope that enriches life. Ann chose the latter. With her
hope, life would continue to be meaningful and ulti-
mately rewarding.

One can continue to see the same sun rising in the
morning and setting in the evening. The world may
not change. It is our perception of the world that
changes. And this can make an enormous difference
in the process of healing.

Knowing an individual's history is essential to
understanding that person. Rarely do we find someone not touched by adverse economic conditions,
bad luck, missed opportunities, family problems,
rejection, phobias, and the like. But what is the use of
being mired in the past? We will never heal if we keep
blaming past experiences and conditions. We should
learn from these experiences without allowing them
to circumscribe our lives today or in the future. We
need hope to maintain a positive outlook.

It may be an oversimplification, but the elderly
often seem to fall into one of two categories. Some

are grateful for life no matter what has happened to them, and radiate peace and joy. Others are angry, bitter, and constantly complaining. It is hope, or its absence, that accounts for these different responses to life's challenges. Without hope, one sees himself or herself as a victim and the other as the enemy. With hope, one has a radically different perspective on everything, because the individual sees the signs of God's presence in life's events.

God is everywhere. If we really believe this, we must conclude that there is no place and no circumstance where God is not present. We ought to be grateful for the sun, air, rain, storms, and everything that goes to make up our experience. By giving thanks we recognize that God is in all things and that God is the source of every healing.

Hope integrates experience. "An organic view of things will make basic conflict impossible," wrote William F. Lynch in his book, *Images of Hope*. It unites us. It makes us whole. It changes our hearts. It effects an inward resurrection and a radical cure. Without hope, life would be unbearable. Samuel Johnson (1709-1784) wrote: "Hope is necessary in every condition. The miseries of poverty, sickness, of captivity, would, without this comfort, be insupportable."

Hope illuminates the myriad facets of our complex problems, and suggests comprehensive solutions at the physical, emotional, intellectual, and spiritual levels. Just as illness affects us on all levels of being, not just the physical, so also its cure

Hope integrates experience.

must involve all aspects of the person. Hope integrates and unites all these levels.

Hope overcomes pessimism and its pernicious consequences. The truth is that we determine our own glorious or flawed destiny through optimism or pessimism. In a sense, our attitude determines our aptitude, and aptitude is a prophecy in progress. The pessimist imagines the worst and generates the conditions for depression; no wonder then if the worst happens. When we don't want to do something, we invent a million different excuses for not doing it.

On the other hand, hope will give us a multitude of reasons for doing it. This optimistic attitude has even biological effects. Dr. Richard J. Davidson, professor of psychology and psychiatry at the University of Wisconsin-Madison, has observed that optimists have higher levels of natural killer-cell activity and are more capable of fighting disease than pessimists.

Great things happen when hearts are transformed; changes are bound to occur on the social level as well as on the personal level. Hope does not only help treat a particular patient or illness, but also considers the root causes of the disease and what can be done to prevent its recurrence; as a result, the general health of the entire population is often improved.

Moreover, hope is always there just for the asking. It is always available to you. Its source never stops flowing. And you never have to pay for it.

Imagine for a moment that the object of your hope is God and the coming of his reign. Would you be able to distinguish your hope from world transformation? Jürgen Moltmann reminds us that "As long as 'every thing' is not 'very good,' the difference between hope and reality remains, and faith remains irreconciled and must press towards the future in hope and suffering."

Hope will help you write your own story.

Hope will help you write your own story. Your life reveals your deepest needs. You should be able to identify these needs—or, at least, the most important one. Would you be willing to spend your life fulfilling this need? What if you're doing something you don't want to do in your own story? You don't want to do bad things in your story. You don't want to do things that are not right for your health. Hope helps you live the personal story you want to write.

Hope keeps faith alive and active in one's personal history as well as in history at large. Hope keeps this history moving onward and upward until all obstacles are overcome. Here are some suggestions to help keep your hope alive, healthy, and efficient:

1. *Discover where your hope is.* What gives you hope? Music? Healthy relationships? Good books? Achieving goals? Prayer? When you find out what it is that gives you hope, take a closer look at it and let it become part of your daily life. Find your magic star. Understand your destiny. Try to reach your full potential. Especially in times of setbacks and difficulties, do what you most like to do. It makes you happy. Happiness and hope go hand in hand.

2. *Set a goal.* Write a mission statement. A mission statement commands goals. These could include writing a book, running a mile every day, building a house, or going back to school. Whatever it is, a goal directs your attention, focuses your intention, and connects your activities with others. Working to

achieve goals engages your talents, exercises your abilities, and builds hope in you, for you, and for others.

3. *Think hope. Speak hope. Act hope.* For ages, wise people have taught that a thought, a word, and an action make things happen. Modern science has endorsed this teaching. Watch out for those negative thoughts. Don't be excessively self-critical. When you need to evaluate your life, learn to do it constructively. Don't say, "Unless I do everything perfectly, I feel I am a failure." Say rather, "My success consists in doing the best that I can do in any given situation." So think, speak, and act in healthy ways.

4. *Plan for the future.* Whether you are healthy or not, planning for the future creates light at the end of the tunnel, generates energy and enthusiasm, and helps you forget mistakes of the past. Plan something—big or small—that gives you satisfaction and joy.

5. *Visualize what you are hoping for.* Have in your mind a clear picture of what you want. Let your wish, desire, intention, attention, passion, and will join forces and concentrate on what you want. Philosopher and psychologist William James (1842-1910) wrote: "There is a law in psychology that if you form a picture in your mind of what you would like to be, and you keep and hold that picture there long

enough, you will soon become exactly as you have been thinking."

6. *Use a resolute and optimistic vocabulary.* Avoid feeble language; instead, use forceful expressions such as "I will," "I shall," "I intend," "I am determined to," etc. In this way you send your subconscious a clear message of serious resolve.

7. *Laugh, laugh, and laugh.* As they say, laughter is the best medicine. Treasure anything that makes you laugh. Collect humorous anecdotes and funny stories. Make a face in front of your mirror. Laughter can succeed when all other things fail. Hope and laughter are very good partners.

8. *Surround yourself with hopeful people.* Make a list of all the people whose attitudes, words, and actions habitually give you a lift. Spend more time with them. Try to give as much hope to them as they provide to you.

9. *Immerse yourself in nature.* Take a walk in the woods or on the seashore or in a city park. Observe how a new bud forms on the seemingly dead branch. Take note of the change of seasons. Expect a sunrise tomorrow as well as a sunset. See how the first flower that blooms heralds the arrival of spring everywhere. Learn hope from nature.

10. *Remember your achievements.* When you are sick, a solid sense of self-worth and the belief that you will contribute something new to the life of your community will help to promote your recovery. And even if you do not achieve great things, remember that you are a child of God, and in this capacity alone, you are entitled to the worth that God's children enjoy.

11. *Take care of yourself physically, emotionally, and spiritually.* Sleep well. Eat well. Exercise. Maintain nurturing and healthy relationships. Read a good book. Detoxify your surroundings, your habits, your lifestyle, your way of thinking, even your religion. "Pray without ceasing" (1 Thess 5:17). Think one hundred years of age. Maybe you won't live that long, but maybe you will—or beyond!

12. *Allow God's Spirit to work in you by transforming you and the entire world.* What do you notice around you? Broken homes. Broken hearts. Broken people. Broken promises. Dysfunctional families. Bankruptcy. Violence. Perverted sex. Murder. Hatred. Prejudice. Compromised ideals. Lost dreams. Lost hopes. The truth is that sick societies generate sick people and sick people generate sick societies. Allow your hope in God to heal society through you.

13. *Take the long view.* If you ask yourself the question, "What will be important to me one hundred years from today?" you will be quick to realize that the list will be remarkably short. Certainly not that trip, or that car, or that house, or even the bank

> We need hope more than anything else.

account. In one hundred years, the only thing that will matter is how you loved God and your neighbor. Hope helps you see this clearly. Learn to live not just for the passing moment, but especially in preparation for what is permanent. Let your theological hope inspire the values that determine your actions.

14. *Remember always to stay in touch with the source of hope.* Remind yourself constantly of the comfort and strength you find in your faith. Remember that God is in charge and that God works in the world through you.

After all is said and done, if you have to choose between being a worldly success or being someone who gives hope, choose the latter. Nothing matters if hope is missing. We need hope more than anything else.

To be fully restored, a person needs a total healing of the spirit, heart, and body, and hope is the best restorative. There is hope.

For Your Reflection and Response

1. Read the story of the people who used to gather around the pool of Beth-zatha (Jn 5). Many of them were "invalids—blind, lame, and paralyzed" people who had hope of a cure. Consider the man who kept his hope alive for thirty-eight years, until he heard the order of Jesus: "Stand up, take your mat and walk." Do you have such a steadfast hope, or are you easily discouraged? Do you find life worth living in spite of all its adversities and disappointments? Do you find comfort and strength in your faith and hope?

2. Have you felt lonely and dispirited when friends fail to visit or call or write? Today, do exactly for others what you have wished for yourself. By giving hope, it will be returned to you many times over.

3. Most of us respond well to a little encouragement. Can you think of something special you can do for someone today, such as tutoring a child, visiting the sick, spending time with the elderly, or adding another person to your circle of friends? Such experiences open up new possibilities and generate the movement of hope

within the life of the individual and the community, and within your own life as well.

4. What are you hoping for? A better world? Eternal life? Heaven on earth? The reign of God? The not yet that becomes the already? Is it important to you to have a sense of purpose in life and a mission? Why? Is your mission part of God's plan for the world? Michelangelo understood that the real danger lay not in having high hopes, but in settling for less. Do you see any application for this insight in your own life?

5. Think of Nelson Mandela, Václav Havel, the former president of Czechoslovakia, Mother Teresa of Calcutta, and actor Christopher Reeve, who is so determined to recover his health. Do you see these individuals as models of hope? Can you name others who, in their respective ways, represent the hope that you believe in? Can you articulate why hope is important for general health in individuals as well as in communities and why it is important even for survival? Do you see hope for reconciliation and peace in the world? What role does hope play in the relationships between individuals and between nations?

AFFIRMATION

Repeat this several times a day.

My hope is my healer and salvation.

PRAYER

Dear God, I am constantly haunted by the "What's next in my life?" question.

If I succeed, I say, "What's next?" If I fail, I say, "What's next?" If everything is rosy, I say, "What's next?" If everything is obscured by the dark of night, I say, "What's next?" If I am healthy, I say, "What's next?" If I am sick, I say, "What's next?" The only time I do not say, "What's next?" is when I am with you.

"Lord, to whom can [I] go?" (Jn 6:68). No more nexts are possible. You are the hope that answers all questions and heals all illnesses. You are my only hope. Amen.

We are not finished beings. Our world is not a finished world. We are in the making, in *via*, on the way, all the time. We continuously progress, but we also have many setbacks and find ourselves stalled from time to time. This is where we need hope in a special way, because hope does the work. Péguy put it so well when he wrote:

> Remarkable virtue of hope, strange mystery, she's not a virtue like the others, she is a virtue against the others.
> She takes the counterposition of all the other virtues. She stands, as it were, against the others, against all the others....

And she stands up to them. To all the virtues. To
all the mysteries....
When they go down she goes up, (she's the one
who's right)....
It's she who causes this reversal....
(Who would have believed that such power, that
supreme power had been given to this little child
Hope)....
She is the only one who does not fool us....
She is the only one who does not disappoint us.

The reason why this little child does not disappoint
us is that hope is a dynamic aspect of God's life within us. God's will for us is to hope for better conditions, a healing, a new life, a new community, even a
new humanity (see Eph 2:15; 4:24). It was a radical
transforming hope which reached us through Jesus
Christ, who was and is, now and forever, the hope for
a total fulfillment of life. God is our hope. Our hope
is God. There is no bigger hope than this hope. The
world belongs to whoever offers it the greater hope,
and no one can give greater hope to the world than
Jesus Christ, the fountain of all hope.

What is so special in Christian hope is that it joins
vision and action together. When the reign of God is
already within us, we cannot but radiate what was

held in hope. People like Mother Teresa of Calcutta, Pope John XXIII, Dorothy Day, Martin Luther King, Jr., and many others were living proof of this truth. Their strength was in hope and trust, for they realized that "In quietness and in trust shall be your strength" (Isa 30:15).

This is why we can fairly say that our healing—personal and societal—depends on God's action and on ours. The fact is that nature can take its course. However, it is also a fact that we can shape nature by releasing its hidden potentialities that were initially put there by the Creator. Since God created us creators, it is our responsibility to work with him toward the creation of the new humanity Paul described.

Hope is an indispensable element in this enterprise, which begins where it ends, from its origin as well as at its destination. No one should miss the great connection that exists between beginnings and endings, between origins and destinations, and between the visible and invisible. They are God's instruments working in our world.

Hope is God in action within us and in the world. By virtue of the creation, incarnation, and redemption, God calls us to renew our earth by investing and engaging, as much as we possibly can, in hope, justice, goodness, loving-kindness, health, and peace. Our hope is a dynamic and committed hope for the new heaven and the new earth. Our hope provides us with the fullness that surpasses what the eye can see and the ear can hear. It allows us to know what is underneath all things—the Presence that is in and about all things.

God has a divine plan for all of us. This plan manifests itself in our community as well as our unique individuality. Hope, then, because of its direct connection with the very source of all life, helps us live God's plan for us—each one of us in true relationship with ourselves and with others—as part of a larger plan, designed not only for our own good and well-being, but for the good and well-being of all. Even when things go wrong and we are mired in adversity, hope will save us. It makes us believe that it is possible to improve our situation and create a better future. Hope, as Gabriel Marcel would say, is the refusal to set limits to the possible. True hope never disappoints us.

Brother Laurence, in *The Practice of the Presence of God*, summarized it well when he wrote: "All things are possible to the one who believes; still more to the one who hopes."